D0887742

pocket posh® king james puzzles

THE OLD TESTAMENT

pocket posh® king james puzzles
✝ THE OLD TESTAMENT

Elder Timothy E. Parker

The **Puzzle Society**™
puzzlesociety.com

Andrews McMeel
Publishing, LLC
Kansas City • Sydney • London

POCKET POSH® KING James PUZZLES:
THE OLD TESTAMENT

Andrews McMeel Publishing, LLC
an Andrews McMeel Universal company
1130 Walnut Street, Kansas City, Missouri 64106

www.andrewsmcmeel.com
www.puzzlesociety.com

11 12 13 14 15 SHZ 10 9 8 7 6 5 4 3 2 1

ISBN: 978-1-4494-0320-1

Illustration by Kate Spain

how to play

"Letter Squares" Puzzles

Arrange the tiles to form a verse from the Holy Bible. The letters inside the squares stay exactly the same. Only the squares are rearranged.

"Verse Decoder" Puzzles

A Verse Decoder is a coded verse from the Holy Bible. Each letter in the puzzle actually represents a different letter. If a coded word was spelled "G A C E C" in the puzzle, you must substitute letters, through trial and error, until the word makes sense.

In the above example "G A C E C" equals "J E S U S." The "G" is actually a "J" in the puzzle, and the "C" is actually an "S." How would you figure that out? The best way to solve these types of puzzles is to first figure out the small words in the puzzle. Helpful hints to get you started are also provided.

"Word Search" Puzzles

Word search puzzles are fun to do and easy to play. Simply find each listed word hidden in the grid. The words may be up, down, forward, backward, or diagonal. They can also overlap, meaning that a single letter can be part of two or more words.

"Column Phrase" Puzzles

Each black square in the puzzle is a space in the verse you are trying to piece together. The letters listed below the puzzle go in the spaces in the column directly above the letters. Letters only go in blank spaces in the column directly above them. However, they need to be placed in the correct squares to reveal the verse and solve the puzzle. The letters always stay in the same column, but their order may need to be shuffled.

Verse Decoder: AMOS 1:6

HINT: In the puzzle below, the letter "K" is actually a "T."

KADY YHLKA KAO MWFZ; UWF KAFOO

_____

KFHTYEFOYYLWTY WU EHXH, HTZ UWF

_____

UWDF, L JLMM TWK KDFT HJHQ KAO

_____

IDTLYAVOTK KAOFOWU; GOBHDYO KAOQ

_____

BHFFLOZ HJHQ BHIKLRO KAO JAWMO

_____

BHIKLRLKQ, KW ZOMLROF KAOV DI KW

_____

OZWV:

_____

3

Crossword: VANITY · By Joseph Mantell

ACROSS

1 Site of a ship's controls
5 Astern
8 Maryland cake ingredient
12 Operatic melody
13 Auto-grille protector
14 "And it is a __ thing that the king requireth" (Dan. 2:11)
15 "... for vanity shall be __" (Job 15:31) (2 words)
18 "As a __ which melteth" (Ps. 58:8)
19 Fermented honey drink
20 Prefix with life or wife
22 Heavenly body
26 Arrogant person
29 "And the men __ up from thence" (Gen. 18:16)
32 Santa __, California
33 "... __ saith the Lord God" (Ezek. 13:8) (4 words)
36 "Who __ to judge?" (2 words)
37 Jamaican citrus fruit
38 "Pharaoh's chariots and his __ hath he cast into the sea" (Ex. 15:4)
39 Gold or silver, e.g.
41 Golf course standard
43 "And saw two ships standing by the __" (Luke 5:2)
46 Initiates a phone call

50 "The Lord knoweth the __" (Ps. 94:11) (3 words)
54 "What time they wax __" (Job 6:17)
55 "Go to the __, thou sluggard" (Prov. 6:6)
56 Dorothy's companion to Oz
57 City in Iowa
58 Negative vote
59 Apply spin

DOWN

1 Exclamations of surprise
2 Ireland, romantically
3 Da Vinci's Mona
4 Xylophone-like instrument
5 Grade-school song start
6 "Cease ye __ man" (Isa. 2:22)
7 Make the wild mild
8 System of beliefs
9 Was on the ballot
10 Circle portion
11 Stinging pest
16 Priest of Israel who looked after Samuel
17 Walks back and forth
21 Air resistance
23 Deli spread (abbr.)
24 Grandson of Adam
25 Without any slack
26 Thailand, once
27 "The __ of the first is Pison" (Gen. 2:11)

4

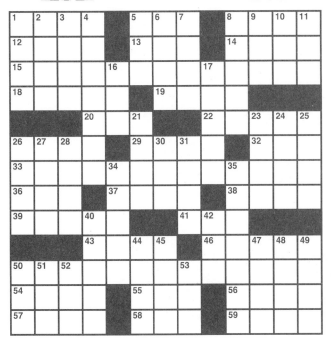

28 Leave out

30 "__ for the light" (Ex. 25:6)

31 Salon sound

34 Russian prison camp

35 Penny-pinchings

40 Grads

42 "Much __ About Nothing"

44 Genghis or Kubla

45 Volcano in Sicily

47 Berserk

48 "Even of __ my people is risen up ..." (Micah 2:8)

49 "If I wash myself with __ water" (Job 9:30)

50 Former U.S. airline

51 Son of Noah

52 Lode product

53 Pig's digs

Word Search: DAVID'S MEN

```
T  K  N  Q  T  Y  J  B  M  H  Z  R  N  R  Y  R  Z
A  Q  K  T  K  V  Q  M  L  A  K  A  N  Y  R  Q  C
J  M  U  Z  Z  I  A  E  C  K  H  C  L  L  F  B  M
I  J  A  S  I  E  L  D  L  A  Q  A  M  M  D  M  E
A  C  Z  H  B  L  M  D  R  H  L  F  R  L  O  C  B
C  D  X  D  S  L  Q  I  J  T  A  E  T  A  F  N  U
E  N  M  T  N  A  T  M  R  N  L  N  G  M  I  R  N
B  E  N  T  K  G  A  K  K  I  X  T  A  L  C  G  N
B  L  W  V  R  I  R  P  P  L  F  G  L  N  K  F  A
I  I  I  Z  H  T  Y  H  K  K  Z  N  E  V  D  R  I
S  A  T  A  K  K  E  L  H  Q  V  K  I  K  T  L  I
G  H  W  M  D  L  Z  A  L  M  R  G  B  V  T  A  Y
G  B  Z  G  E  D  I  N  A  N  A  H  A  K  T  N  T
R  A  R  T  H  R  I  R  L  F  K  K  N  T  F  D  J
D  V  G  L  U  V  N  H  W  W  D  Z  I  M  T  M  T
M  X  K  J  W  X  B  E  N  A  I  A  H  K  M  K  N
G  L  D  E  B  O  T  B  R  P  Y  P  L  N  J  Q  F
```

ABIEL	HIDDAI	OBED
AHIAM	IGAL	SHAMA
BENAIAH	ITTAI	SIBBECAI
ELHANAN	JASIEL	URIAH
ELIAHBA	MAHARAI	UZZIA
ELIPHELET	MEBUNNAI	ZALMON
HANAN	NAHARI	

Multiple Choice

1   How many years did Noah live?

    A   950 years
    B   750 years
    C   890 years
    D   670 years

2   When Moses left Egypt for the promised
land, whose bones did he take along?

    A   Jacob's
    B   Joseph's
    C   Noah's
    D   Abraham's

3   Who built an altar and called it
Jehovahnissi, or "The Lord is my banner"?

    A   Abraham
    B   Noah
    C   Moses
    D   Aaron

Letter Squares: DEUTERONOMY 1:32

NO	DID	E LI	NG	E V E	THI	ORD	GOD
T B	UR	TH	YE	E L	IS	TH	YET
YO	IN	,					

Multiple Choice

1 While being pursued by his enemies, whose hair became caught in an oak tree?

    A Absalom
    B Jonathan
    C Solomon
    D Adonijah

2 Who lied to Ahab about the result of a battle?

    A Iddo
    B Micaiah
    C Micah
    D Azariah

3 Whose brothers were imprisoned after being falsely accused of being spies in Egypt?

    A Job's
    B Jacob's
    C Joseph's
    D Joshua's

Multiple Choice

1 What judge built an altar and called it Jehovahshalom, or "The Lord is peace"?

    A Othniel
    B Gideon
    C Moses
    D Aaron

2 Whose lips were touched by a coal from the altar in the temple?

    A Aaron
    B Isaiah
    C Jeremiah
    D Elijah

3 Who went mad as a result of a prideful heart?

    A Nehum
    B Pedaiah
    C Nebuchadnezzar
    D Jeroham

Word Search: **QUEEN ESTHER**

```
L  P  C  S  H  A  A  S  H  G  A  Z  T  N  J  M
H  L  O  Z  G  Q  R  H  R  E  H  T  S  E  T  M
V  O  N  T  Q  N  I  G  R  I  V  M  S  L  S  P
C  I  C  C  R  D  I  D  Q  C  Q  T  Y  E  A  C
M  N  U  D  X  L  G  N  N  N  F  N  C  L  R  J
B  T  B  B  M  K  S  R  E  I  T  I  A  O  R  S
J  M  I  K  E  O  J  E  G  V  P  C  W  J  U  Q
Z  E  N  G  D  A  R  L  C  S  E  N  H  R  R  J
S  N  E  M  E  Y  U  N  L  N  R  G  E  N  Z  B
T  T  S  Z  T  W  P  T  I  V  I  U  Q  G  M  G
N  S  Q  L  P  D  M  R  Y  N  S  R  C  T  D  M
A  V  N  Q  O  R  P  W  R  A  G  M  P  Z  Z  Q
V  L  B  L  D  O  F  X  H  Y  D  F  Y  Q  R  M
R  H  W  M  A  V  R  A  H  A  D  A  S  S  A  H
E  W  N  Z  X  A  D  B  A  N  Q  U  E  T  T  M
S  R  J  R  K  F  Q  D  D  E  S  A  E  L  P  Q
```

ADOPTED	EVENING	PLEASED
AHASUERUS	FAVOR	PRINCES
BANQUET	GIFTS	SERVANTS
BEAUTY	HADASSAH	SHAASHGAZ
CONCUBINES	MORNING	SPICES
CROWN	OINTMENTS	VIRGIN
ESTHER	PALACE	

Letter Squares: DEUTERONOMY 6:4

| E | L | RD : | TH | ORD | EL : | SRA | IS | R G |

| R , | OD | HEA | OU | LO O | I | ONE |

Verse Decoder: EZRA 10:8

HINT: In the puzzle below, the letter "Q" is actually a "T."

SEL QUSQ NUIKIYZYV NIDCL EIQ TIOY

NMQUME QUVYY LSWK, STTIVLMER QI QUY

TIDEKYC IP QUY FVMETYK SEL QUY

YCLYVK, SCC UMK KDGKQSETY KUIDCL GY

PIVPYMQYL, SEL UMOKYCP KYFSVSQYL

PVIO QUY TIERVYRSQMIE IP QUIKY QUSQ

USL GYYE TSVVMYL SNSW.

13

Crossword: OLD TESTAMENT BOOKS · By Thomas W. Schier

ACROSS

1 Water-to-wine town
5 "... and it shall be thy __" (Ex. 29:26)
9 Noah's son
12 Sensory stimulant
13 Together, in music
14 Honest president?
15 Two OT books (3 words)
18 "And God __ the firmament" (Gen. 1:7)
19 "As an eagle stirreth up her __" (Deut. 32:11)
20 Two OT books (3 words)
25 Jai __
26 Drop of gel
27 Señor on the Sullivan show
30 Perfumed ointment
35 Spanish aunt
37 *Night* author Wiesel
38 Two OT books (3 words)
44 This, señora
45 Mythical queen of Carthage
46 Two OT books (3 words)
52 Actress Zadora
53 *Green Mansions* girl
54 OT book
55 French possessive
56 Slangy snack
57 Lyricist Lorenz

DOWN

1 Runner Sebastian
2 Wood-dressing tool (variant)
3 "... will not fail thee, __ forsake thee" (Josh. 1:5)
4 Biblical language
5 National zoo animal
6 Number next to a plus sign
7 Wish one could take back
8 ___-Mex food
9 Mythical hell
10 Mistreatment
11 River of Thrace or hostess Perle
16 Checkup sound
17 Yoko __
20 "... with the __ of an ass ..." (Judg. 15:16)
21 Grand __ Opry
22 One of the Bobbsey twins
23 Skip, as a stone on water
24 Cable station
28 LAX guesstimate
29 Go against God's commandments
31 Hanukkah centerpiece
32 1996 Olympic torch lighter
33 "Ye shall not surely __" (Gen. 3:4)
34 Serpentine swimmer
36 Uncle Fester or Morticia
38 WWII vehicles

14

1	2	3	4		5	6	7	8		9	10	11
12					13					14		
15				16					17			
			18						19			
20	21	22					23	24				
25						26						
27				28	29		30		31	32	33	34
			35		36			37				
38	39	40	41				42	43				
44					45							
46			47	48				49	50	51		
52			53					54				
55			56					57				

39 Actor Davis
40 Kett and James
41 ___-di-dah
42 Leah's daughter
43 Say a bit more

47 Flying fish-eater
48 Brazilian city, for short
49 Actress Thurman
50 Rocky pinnacle
51 FDR's successor

15

Multiple Choice

1 When God said, "Before I formed thee
   in the belly I knew thee." Who was He
   speaking to?

   A Jeremiah
   B John
   C Jehoshaphat
   D Joshua

2 Who slept at Bethel and dreamed about
   angels?

   A Esau
   B Eli
   C Joseph
   D Jacob

3 What boy was awakened out of his sleep
   by the voice of God?

   A Samuel
   B Aaron
   C David
   D Josiah

1	2	3	4		5	6	7	8		9	10	11
12					13					14		
15				16					17			
			18						19			
20	21	22					23	24				
25						26						
27				28	29		30		31	32	33	34
			35		36			37				
38	39	40	41				42	43				
44					45							
46			47	48					49	50	51
52				53					54			
55				56					57			

39 Actor Davis
40 Kett and James
41 ___-di-dah
42 Leah's daughter
43 Say a bit more

47 Flying fish-eater
48 Brazilian city, for short
49 Actress Thurman
50 Rocky pinnacle
51 FDR's successor

Multiple Choice

1 When God said, "Before I formed thee in the belly I knew thee." Who was He speaking to?

    A Jeremiah
    B John
    C Jehoshaphat
    D Joshua

2 Who slept at Bethel and dreamed about angels?

    A Esau
    B Eli
    C Joseph
    D Jacob

3 What boy was awakened out of his sleep by the voice of God?

    A Samuel
    B Aaron
    C David
    D Josiah

Word Search: **ALTAR SITES**

```
K  P  Y  K  F  G  M  R  E  P  H  I  D  I  M  P  W
M  H  V  F  H  I  N  T  J  S  U  C  S  A  M  A  D
B  G  M  A  Z  F  T  L  N  T  N  C  T  R  F  M  W
M  H  M  P  M  Q  L  X  C  K  N  Q  A  C  X  M  N
B  A  E  N  V  C  V  X  R  O  N  Z  R  A  W  Q  R
R  H  B  E  E  R  S  H  E  B  A  D  A  N  J  G  H
N  H  E  R  O  M  H  B  L  X  J  N  R  A  L  Y  A
S  K  L  C  C  T  I  Y  V  V  B  W  A  A  Z  K  R
H  Z  H  J  Z  G  N  C  C  K  K  M  K  N  J  Y  H
E  S  H  E  T  P  A  T  X  W  S  C  R  P  D  M  P
C  M  A  W  B  R  B  R  M  N  Y  F  V  J  L  J  O
H  A  F  M  M  R  J  E  E  J  H  K  H  N  E  R  W
E  M  G  E  A  M  O  H  T  V  L  A  L  T  I  J  M
M  R  L  V  C  R  T  N  V  H  F  A  I  X  F  W  M
H  E  M  M  N  A  I  H  K  H  E  Q  B  R  Q  R  T
V  R  J  Q  J  F  X  A  X  F  Y  L  N  E  O  V  N
M  B  V  H  T  M  B  H  G  H  E  A  V  E  N  M  L
```

ARARAT	EBAL	MOREH
ATHENS	FIELD	MORIAH
BEERSHEBA	GIBEON	OPHRAH
BETHEL	HEAVEN	RAMAH
CANAAN	HEBRON	REPHIDIM
CARMEL	MAMRE	SAMARIA
DAMASCUS	MIZPEH	SHECHEM

Column Phrase: PSALMS 37:39

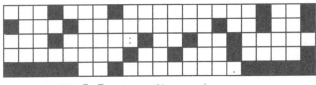

```
      O F      N     I
  T E      O E      T H O U H I    T    O F
S T H   N H T H S A E V A T E    T    M E
B U T E L R R D T R L U T S S I S H O I
T H R E T G I G H I O E B L E O N I E F R
```

18

Multiple Choice

1   Who was the first man to have more than one wife?

    A   Adam
    B   Abel
    C   Cain
    D   Lamech

2   Which book of the Bible begins, "How doth the city sit solitary, that was full of people!"?

    A   Isaiah
    B   Lamentations
    C   Daniel
    D   Ezekiel

3   Who was married to Jezebel?

    A   Agag
    B   Agee
    C   Ader
    D   Ahab

Multiple Choice

1 What prophet refused to use anointing oils during a mourning period of three weeks?

    A Nathan
    B Joel
    C Daniel
    D Isaiah

2 To avoid the wrath of Saul, who hid in caves?

    A David
    B Jonathan
    C Solomon
    D Samuel

3 The men of Israel laughed at whose decree for a Passover celebration?

    A Isaiah
    B Hezekiah
    C Saul
    D David

Letter Squares: EXODUS 12:47

ATI	EP	OF	ALL	E C	TH	ON	AEL
ISR	IT.	SH	ONG	REG	ALL	KE	

<table>
<tr><td></td><td></td><td></td><td></td><td></td><td></td><td></td><td></td></tr>
<tr><td></td><td></td><td></td><td></td><td></td><td></td><td></td></tr>
</table>

Word Search: ISRAEL'S ENEMIES

```
F  W  N  S  E  T  I  H  S  A  G  R  I  G  H
D  R  N  K  A  D  M  O  N  I  T  E  S  G  I
X  A  A  B  N  O  L  Y  B  A  B  A  E  W  T
F  S  M  N  G  B  F  M  K  F  H  N  T  T  T
B  E  I  O  Q  O  B  L  M  O  L  A  I  M  I
O  T  H  M  R  D  L  F  R  T  G  K  S  L  T
N  I  A  O  N  I  P  I  G  E  S  H  U  R  E
E  Z  Z  D  B  K  T  H  A  T  K  Q  B  R  S
B  Z  Y  E  M  E  K  E  C  T  Q  G  E  T  A
I  I  N  F  S  E  N  T  S  T  H  T  J  V  G
B  N  Y  A  L  L  P  A  M  M  O  N  V  H  N
H  E  Z  A  I  Y  X  X  A  T  R  I  K  M  Q
S  K  M  T  G  D  M  G  N  N  T  M  T  M  Z
I  A  Q  E  Z  F  I  M  C  E  A  H  K  F  D
B  R  L  N  G  M  M  M  S  C  L  C  G  C  R
```

AHIMAN
AMALEK
AMMON
AMORITES
ANAK
AVVITES
BABYLON

CANAAN
EDOM
EGYPT
GESHUR
GIRGASHITES
GOLIATH
HITTITES

HORITES
ISHBIBENOB
JEBUSITES
KADMONITES
KENIZZITES
MIDIAN

Verse Decoder: EXODUS 6:1

HINT: In the puzzle below, the letter "P" is actually an "E."

YWPX YWP KABM OVJM TXYA IAOPO, XAN

_____

OWVKY YWAT OPP NWVY J NJKK MA YA

_____

RWVBVAW: SAB NJYW V OYBAXD WVXM

_____

OWVKK WP KPY YWPI DA, VXM NJYW V

_____

OYBAXD WVXM OWVKK WP MBJGP YWPI

_____

ATY AS WJO KVXM.

_____

23

Crossword: PRAISES · By Rowan Millson

ACROSS

1 Windbag?
5 "... of wines on the __ well refined" (Isa. 25:6)
9 "Because thou saidst, __, against my sanctuary" (Eze. 25:3)
12 Balm ingredient, perhaps
13 First gardener?
14 Brooklyn Dodger sobriquet
15 "And the __ man shall be brought down" (Isa. 5:15)
16 Org. for Senator Glenn
17 Ginger __ (soda choice)
18 "Get thee __" (Matt. 16:23) (3 words)
21 Tree with tough, useful wood
22 "Ten-__!"
23 __ chi (martial art)
26 Direction of Nod from Eden
29 Part of the mezzanine
32 "Get wisdom, get __" (Prov. 4:5)
35 Ill-mannered type
36 "... and his commandments are __" (Ps. 111:7)
37 Floor cover
38 Pastureland
40 Boston party drink
42 "And I will get them __ ..." (Zeph. 3:19) (3 words)
49 Gone for the day
50 "... and they could not __ him" (Matt. 17:16)
51 "... thou shalt not lift up any iron __ upon them" (Deut. 27:5)
52 "I am the voice of __ crying in the wilderness" (John 1:23)
53 Food morsels
54 He lived for 905 years
55 For every
56 Yo-yos and pogo sticks
57 Descartes or Russo

DOWN

1 "Behold the __ of God" (John 1:29)
2 "Golden" role for Peter Fonda
3 Father of Japheth, Ham, and Shem
4 Three wishes giver of myth
5 Asia, for one
6 Mild cheese
7 Comfort
8 Good kind of hit
9 Slaughterhouse
10 Hawaiian dance
11 End of The Lord's Prayer
19 NY Met, e.g.
20 "__ Lang Syne"
23 Place for a soak?
24 *Wheel of Fortune* selection
25 Golden calf adorer, for one
27 R-V connection?
28 Sourness
30 Bearded antelope

1	2	3	4		5	6	7	8		9	10	11
12					13					14		
15					16					17		
18				19					20			
			21					22				
23	24	25		26		27	28		29		30	31
32			33					34				
35					36					37		
		38		39			40		41			
42	43				44	45				46	47	48
49				50						51		
52				53						54		
55				56						57		

31 "... is there any taste in the white of an __?" (Job 6:6)

33 "Able was I __ saw Elba" (2 words)

34 "For ye have __ of patience" (Heb. 10:36)

39 Broad necktie

41 "And it came to pass __ seven days" (Gen. 7:10)

42 Certain ship deck

43 Ancient alphabetic symbol

44 Continental currency

45 Pretentious, in a way

46 Tip-top

47 "Praise ye him, sun and __" (Ps. 148:3)

48 "Give me children, or __ I die" (Gen. 30:1)

Letter Squares: JONAH 1:15

NAH	:		UP	OOK	FOR	T	H	Y	T	HE
TH	SEA	O T	SO		CAS	THE		JO	, A	
ND	IM	INT								

Multiple Choice

1 Othniel was the first judge of Israel. Who followed him as the second?

    A Samuel
    B Jehu
    C Deborah
    D Ehud

2 Which father of twelve sons had a father who became blind in his old age?

    A Jacob
    B Abraham
    C Isaac
    D Job

3 Visitors to which city struck sinful men with blindness?

    A Ephesus
    B Dan
    C Sodom
    D Gomorrah

Word Search: NOAH'S ARK

```
N  R  W  V  Y  Z  H  X  K  W  N  X  R  H  C
N  L  B  N  T  E  W  R  R  M  I  Y  D  V  R
L  K  T  C  L  K  A  A  S  G  E  N  C  Q  K
W  R  B  T  Q  S  V  B  F  L  J  H  D  D  N
Y  N  T  M  H  E  R  L  J  R  W  L  S  O  H
L  A  G  A  N  B  O  R  E  S  K  O  B  V  W
C  R  O  P  N  O  F  T  V  E  R  G  F  E  R
Z  N  M  D  D  R  A  Y  N  D  A  P  N  M  F
N  N  N  N  T  W  T  M  X  I  T  H  R  J  K
P  I  T  C  H  D  O  O  F  S  L  T  A  X  L
B  C  O  V  E  N  A  N  T  L  A  E  I  D  R
K  M  J  M  W  D  C  R  M  R  R  H  N  K  P
L  R  L  B  Q  L  O  W  A  K  C  P  B  T  R
B  V  K  W  I  F  E  O  W  I  N  A  O  R  H
T  H  W  S  M  O  O  R  R  K  N  J  W  R  R
```

ALTAR	FOWLS	ROOMS
CATTLE	JAPHETH	SHEM
COVENANT	NOAH'S ARK	SIDES
DOOR	PITCH	WATER
DOVE	RAIN	WIFE
FLOOD	RAINBOW	WINDOW
FOOD	RAVEN	

Multiple Choice

1   Which two tribes of Israel were
    descended from an Egyptian woman?

    A   Reuben and Simeon
    B   Manasseh and Ephraim
    C   Dan and Naphtali
    D   Benjamin and Judah

2   Who impressed the Queen of Sheba with
    his wisdom when she visited him?

    A   Daniel
    B   Solomon
    C   King Saul
    D   Job

3   Jemima was whose daughter?

    A   Hosea
    B   Moses
    C   Job
    D   Noah

Multiple Choice

1   Who rebuked David for committing murder and having an adulterous affair with Bathsheba?

    A Samuel
    B Saul
    C Uriah
    D Nathan

2   How long did it take Abraham to travel to the place where he would offer Isaac as a sacrifice?

    A Three days
    B Three weeks
    C One month
    D One year

3   Who ran away from Queen Jezebel and heard God's voice?

    A Elisha
    B Elijah
    C David
    D Gomer

Column Phrase: PSALMS 34:19

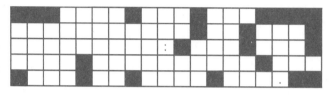

```
A O U H I C F I I V E M O T H L H E
L O R M T E O L T N S B E T E T H E
R F F D A O Y U S H E R U A L T H I M
    I G   D T   A R E     T H
    N E   O         F
```

Word Search: THE FIRST COUPLE

```
F  Y  B  N  S  E  R  P  E  N  T  L  E  Y  C  D
F  F  D  E  S  R  U  C  J  R  P  V  K  T  G  D
T  T  R  L  B  E  G  U  I  L  E  D  V  I  W  X
P  R  N  U  M  P  Y  V  H  D  C  R  R  R  Z  N
P  L  E  F  I  Y  B  E  N  N  N  A  Y  U  F  Y
N  N  N  E  T  T  M  A  B  L  F  O  I  P  C  X
R  K  M  I  S  X  M  C  D  O  M  H  H  N  Y  H
H  C  M  H  K  A  D  H  P  D  S  B  Z  S  H  T
Y  N  C  W  D  B  X  E  X  Z  P  I  X  I  I  J
E  K  G  A  Z  L  P  R  X  G  L  V  D  G  L  P
T  M  I  N  N  E  L  U  C  M  P  D  L  S  C  T
N  L  H  C  M  B  Q  B  Y  N  E  H  R  L  Q  S
J  N  O  T  T  A  Y  I  T  K  B  E  A  N  Q  A
Q  Q  N  K  F  G  Y  M  E  N  V  Y  N  H  P  E
L  A  R  U  T  A  N  L  Y  I  R  D  G  D  F  K
T  N  T  R  E  U  P  H  R  A  T  E  S  D  W  X
```

ABEL	DISOBEY	NATURAL
ADAM AND EVE	EAST	PISHON
BEGUILED	ENMITY	PURITY
CAIN	EUPHRATES	RIVERS
CHERUBIM	FRUIT	SERPENT
CLAY	GIHON	TREES
CURSED	HIDDEKEL	

Verse Decoder: GENESIS 43:2

HINT: In the puzzle below, the letter "Y" is actually an "E."

FUC BM WFEY ML JFHH, QZYU MZYK ZFC

YFMYU GJ MZY WLDU QZBWZ MZYK ZFC

VDLGXZM LGM LR YXKJM, MZYBD RFMZYD

HFBC GUML MZYE, XL FXFBU, VGK GH F

NBMMNY RLLC.

Crossword: HONOR • By Joseph Mantell

ACROSS

1 In baseball, it's grand
5 Health resort
8 Son of Noah
12 Verdi opera
13 Be unwell
14 "Then the king arose, and __ his garments" (2 Sam. 13:31)
15 "A __ retaineth honour: and strong men retain riches" (Prov. 11:16) (2 words)
18 Brazilian dance
19 Head for the heavens
20 "And it came to pass at the __ of forty days" (Gen. 8:6)
22 "The __ saith, 'It is not in me'" (Job 28:14)
26 "At the __ it biteth like a serpent" (Prov. 23:32)
29 Seep
32 Baseball manager Piniella
33 "I will speak __ honour of thy majesty" (Ps. 145:5) (3 words)
36 Woman's garment
37 Make over
38 Commonly held false notion
39 Dolphin detector
41 Janitor's implement
43 Bag style
46 Called one's bluff

50 "__ honour come of thee" (1 Chron. 29:12) (3 words)
54 Muffin spread
55 Fraternity letter
56 Greek portico
57 Desires
58 Apply bread to gravy
59 "For my yoke is __, and my burden is light" (Matt. 11:30)

DOWN

1 Droops
2 Former Italian currency
3 Garden of Eden tender
4 Shakespeare character
5 __ Paulo (Brazilian city)
6 Name of 12 popes
7 Likewise
8 "Blessed shall be thy basket and thy __" (Deut. 28:5)
9 Brother of Japheth
10 Notable time period
11 "Young __ likewise exhort to be sober minded" (Titus 2:6)
16 Author Fleming
17 Long-legged bird
21 Chief official of Venice or Genoa
23 Tactical maneuver
24 Show off
25 Fall silent
26 High-arced tennis returns
27 Hair style

1	2	3	4		5	6	7		8	9	10	11
12					13				14			
15				16				17				
18						19						
			20		21			22		23	24	25
26	27	28			29	30	31			32		
33				34				35				
36				37				38				
39			40				41	42				
		43		44	45		46		47	48	49	
50	51	52				53						
54				55				56				
57				58				59				

28 Hall-of-famer Musial
30 Like Methuselah
31 Certain lens
34 Misplay
35 Negotiation situation
40 One of the Three Musketeers
42 Keats's forte
44 Waiter's mainstay

45 Sound return
47 Pro __ (proportionately)
48 He lived for 905 years
49 June 6, 1944
50 Man-to-be
51 Matador's encouragement
52 Countdown starter
53 Body joint

35

KING JAMES PUZZLES (30)

Letter Squares: JONAH 4:4

ORD	OES	HOU	LL	T T	, D	AID	THE
E L	BE	WE	RY?	TH	ANG	TO	N S

Word Search: WELLS AND POOLS

```
R  H  Z  R  H  E  Y  T  M  K  V  V  K  N  N
D  A  N  M  R  N  I  S  R  A  E  L  I  L  M
O  O  C  M  X  H  D  R  A  G  O  N  N  L  N
R  T  J  X  T  A  J  B  C  D  N  T  G  A  Q
A  H  G  W  G  K  N  Z  B  K  K  O  S  H  J
H  P  D  H  M  K  N  O  E  B  I  G  H  A  K
N  E  D  F  T  O  L  W  L  M  W  B  M  I  T
A  N  H  L  R  R  C  K  A  T  A  R  P  R  G
I  N  G  B  J  E  N  D  W  Y  W  O  P  O  K
R  Y  E  L  G  A  S  M  S  R  K  M  L  I  M
A  H  V  Q  E  E  C  R  T  E  F  M  Z  I  L
M  N  N  S  H  W  E  O  L  E  W  M  X  O  S
A  B  E  T  L  W  L  L  B  B  K  L  W  V  C
S  K  E  P  O  K  B  M  I  S  M  E  D  H  V
Z  B  N  T  H  A  R  A  M  M  R  V  N  H  T
```

BEER
BETHESDA
DRAGON
ELIM
ENHAKKORE
ESEK
GIBEON

GIHON
HAROD
HEBRON
ISRAEL
JACOBS
KINGS
LAHAIROI

LOWER
MARAH
NEPHTOAH
SAMARIA
SILOAM
TOWERS

Multiple Choice

1 What did the Lord rain down upon
   Sodom and Gomorrah?

   A Frogs
   B Locusts
   C Fire and brimstone
   D Thunder and lightning

2 Jacob had twelve sons. In order, what
   number was Joseph?

   A 11th
   B 9th
   C 4th
   D 12th

3 Which of these men followed in their
   father's footsteps by calling their wife
   their sister?

   A Adam
   B Isaac
   C Abel
   D Moses

Letter Squares: MALACHI 2:1

| NO | E | P | STS | W, | , | T | OU . | HIS | FO |
| AND | CO | NDM | MMA | R | Y | O Y | IS | RIE |
| ENT |

Multiple Choice

1 Out of these four sons of Jacob, who was the only one born in Canaan?

    A Judah
    B Benjamin
    C Joseph
    D Levi

2 Who as a child fought and defeated the giant Goliath?

    A Samuel
    B Jesse
    C David
    D Saul

3 Which of these prophets had two sons named Shear-jashub and Maher-shalal-hash-baz?

    A Jeremiah
    B Ezekiel
    C Isaiah
    D Habakkuk

Word Search: ABRAHAM'S PROGENY

```
L H Z D Z T M H G J F N N H H F J K
M D B G L I T M I D I A N A R W R K
M I H N C Z M D E D A N N N K N A X
L N Z D R J P R L P L E N O N L D P
Z A R Z V Y R N A P M N P C T N E X
G H L E A M H S I N I Z A H J D K R
J A P M L H L X C J R F B H R Q L Q
F T L Q T H Y J X L U G T V S A L K
L H L F K P L Z Q N H H K N M K I D
M Q X G G C F M H I S J G X L V O M
L K G W Z Z I N M H S H U A H L H J
V Y M D X M E R N X A Y M D Y E Z D
Y G G C M B A M H G R M K Z Z X B P
B L B U A C Y A A C G M M R K Z T M
R L E J L C L T B K F L O A H D W R
T L O B W E V D E X R N C R H F F G
R T J R H P T N H T W T D L Q S L D
H N G S D Q N M S Q L D Z E R E P W
```

ASSHURIM
CARMI
DEDAN
EPHRAIM
HANOCH
HEZRON
ISHMAEL

JOKSHAN
KEDAR
LEUMMIM
MIDIAN
MIZZAH
NAHATH
NEBAJOTH

PEREZ
SHAMMAH
SHEBA
SHELAH
SHUAH
ZIMRAN

Verse Decoder: GENESIS 28:12

HINT: In the puzzle below, the letter "H" is actually an "A."

HSC GQ CWQHJQC, HSC RQGNBC H BHCCQW

OQX DT NS XGQ QHWXG, HSC XGQ XNT NM

LX WQHEGQC XN GQHYQS: HSC RQGNBC

XGQ HSAQBO NM ANC HOEQSCLSA HSC

CQOEQSCLSA NS LX.

Letter Squares: MALACHI 3:6

| AM | | NO | T ; | | I | | NGE | RD , | THE | CHA |

| FOR | | I | | LO |

```
┌────┬────┬────┬────┬────┬────┬────┬────┐
│    │    │    │    │    │    │    │    │
├────┼────┼────┼────┴────┴────┴────┴────┘
│    │    │    │
└────┴────┴────┘
```

Crossword: KNOWLEDGE • By Joseph Mantell

ACROSS

1 Mild punishment, when applied to the wrist
5 Author Fleming
8 Church recess
12 Source of Samson's strength
13 __ Jo (Olympic athlete)
14 Horse coloring
15 "Take you wise men, and __" (Deut. 1:13)
18 Finger-lickin' good
19 Buckeye State
20 End of a British alphabet
22 Boardroom easel display
26 Adolescent's bane
29 Informal agreement
32 Grazing land
33 "__ God knowledge?" (Job 21:22) (3 words)
36 Small fruit seed
37 Scandinavian saga
38 Inquires
39 "... they cast four anchors out of the __" (Acts 27:29)
41 "Whereas thou __ been forsaken and hated" (Isa. 60:15)
43 Above
46 Supreme Ross
50 "But of the tree of the knowledge __" (Gen. 2:17) (4 words)
54 Stead

55 Egg cells
56 "And Jacob said, __ me this day thy birthright" (Gen. 25:31) (4 words)
57 Farmer's place, in song
58 Confederate soldier, for short
59 A low card

DOWN

1 "And Miriam was __ out from the camp" (Num. 12:15)
2 Turner of films
3 Helps out
4 Knotted snack
5 No __, ands, or buts
6 Certain choir member
7 Father of Japheth, Ham, and Shem
8 Intense feeling of love
9 Maui finger food
10 Start for Diego or Francisco
11 MIT grad, perhaps
16 Type of bread
17 "... and the darkness he called __" (Gen. 1:5)
21 Couple
23 "__, poor Yorick"
24 Legendary actor Gregory
25 Exclamations of surprise
26 Egyptian cobras
27 Bill in a restaurant
28 Back of the neck

44

1	2	3	4		5	6	7		8	9	10	11
12					13				14			
15				16				17				
18						19						
			20		21			22		23	24	25
26	27	28			29	30	31			32		
33				34					35			
36				37					38			
39			40				41	42				
		43		44	45		46		47	48	49	
50	51	52				53						
54					55				56			
57					58				59			

30 "The __ of all flesh is come before me" (Gen. 6:13)

31 Indian nurse

34 Slow, in music

35 Most effortless

40 French artist Dufy

42 "The Lord shall __ to me another son" (Gen. 30:24)

44 Offensive smell

45 Surface

47 Declare as true

48 World's longest river

49 Colleague

50 "And Noah was five hundred years __" (Gen. 5:32)

51 Exclamation of disgust

52 Mousse alternative

53 Get the bad guy

Word Search: CITIES OF JUDAH

```
H Y W N M O L A D A H T Y M K Q X M
B M X F V T J E R U S A L E M G K E
J B R F S T D N X Q D C V G F T L L
N M M H M I H L I H S Y K J X G Q E
M L E Q M R C G R D A L O T L E H T
T M B O T C Q N X Z N N L N G V A L
A A N B R Y F H D M B T R A H J D E
K A N N M K K M B T I R L O F C A B
H B T N V J E B B N Z K D Q Z V D A
N W E B A J P D J L I J C L D A A O
W R R A M M R M E Z O D L W G N H T
C D Z N L B D L L S T R N B R Y C H
Y R R I G O F A J R H V R W M M N V
M R X N P K T Q M Y I F J W Q R O C
W G N T V H M H L V A N V M U K R G
M P K W K A Z X G B H N P G Y L B R
C G B P M K B A A L A H A N P K E L
T T N A T P D B T B N J B M F M H X
```

ADADAH
AMAM
BAALAH
BEALOTH
BIZIOTHIAN
DIMONAH
ELTOLAD

HAZOR
HEBRON
JAGUR
JERUSALEM
KEDESH
LEBAOTH
MADMANNA

MOLADAH
SHEMA
SHILHIM
TELEM
ZIKLAG
ZIPH

Multiple Choice

1   Whose mother died while giving birth
    to him?

    A   Judah
    B   Benjamin
    C   Levi
    D   Reuben

2   Whose father was the wicked king Ahaz?

    A   Nahum
    B   Hezekiah
    C   Malachi
    D   Zechariah

3   Joseph allowed his father and brothers to
    dwell in which land?

    A   Moab
    B   Goshen
    C   Beulah
    D   Canaan

Column Phrase: PSALMS 103:12

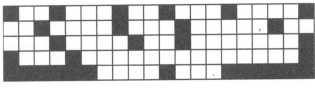

```
            R     H     W
   A     T R   N S   E E   I     T
   S R   R A T H O S G T H E S O A E D
F O S F F O F A A M E U S S S T O S S
I A U R H A M R T H E R R E M E V N S O
```

Multiple Choice

1 Which prophet declared that the people robbed God in their tithes and offerings?

    A Zephaniah
    B Malachi
    C Micah
    D Hosea

2 Who was the brother of Rebekah and father of Rachel and Leah?

    A Laadan
    B Kohath
    C Laban
    D Lamech

3 Samuel anointed what shepherd boy, the youngest of eight sons, in front of his brothers?

    A Josiah
    B David
    C Joseph
    D Solomon

Multiple Choice

1 What man of the military conquered 31 kings?

    A Samson
    B David
    C Joshua
    D Nimrod

2 Who does the Bible say carried a staff that was as big as a weaver's beam?

    A Moses
    B Goliath
    C David
    D Joseph

3 What was the penalty in Israel for disobeying a priest?

    A Imprisonment for one year
    B Daily confessions for one year
    C Death
    D Daily sacrifices for one year

Letter Squares: JOEL 1:15

FOR	HAN	Y !	E	D	LO	D .		DA	S F
OF	AT	THE	IS	ALA	THE		TH	OR
AY	RD

51

Word Search: JEWISH KINGS

```
P  T  R  G  H  R  Z  H  M  A  H  A  Z  I  A  H  W
P  W  D  I  G  H  A  A  R  E  Z  J  X  G  M  T  T
G  J  R  P  G  A  H  B  E  G  H  R  V  R  P  P  R
N  M  W  Z  K  J  A  C  T  H  X  N  J  G  C  F  L
O  Q  V  T  Y  I  O  K  N  R  S  O  E  G  P  F  Z
J  J  J  B  D  B  H  K  X  C  T  O  V  M  T  B  W
H  O  N  E  V  A  E  Q  B  H  M  D  H  R  P  W  M
A  R  M  Y  H  B  J  T  A  H  A  I  K  E  Z  E  H
I  A  L  C  A  U  T  M  P  E  K  A  H  I  A  H  M
K  M  N  H  J  J  G  R  T  G  C  B  N  X  D  I  L
E  R  A  B  G  H  L  V  M  W  Y  B  A  M  K  V  P
D  X  D  T  J  E  H  O  S  H  A  P  H  A  T  P  Y
E  B  A  D  H  E  S  S  A  N  A  M  I  T  S  R  Y
Z  A  V  H  G  R  G  P  N  E  R  O  Y  K  K  H  J
Q  D  I  J  Y  V  M  R  L  D  H  N  M  J  C  B  A
P  A  D  Z  T  B  N  A  P  E  R  L  T  X  P  B  M
N  N  Z  J  V  C  H  C  J  Z  K  Q  M  N  D  T  V
```

ABIJAH	HOSHEA	MANASSEH
AHAB	JEHOAHAZ	MENHEM
AHAZIAH	JEHOIAKIM	NADAB
BAASHA	JEHOSHAPHAT	OMRI
DAVID	JEHU	PEKAHIAH
ELAH	JORAM	ZEDEKIAH
HEZEKIAH	JOTHAM	

Verse Decoder: ISAIAH 1:4

HINT: In the puzzle below, the letter "V" is actually an "A."

VZ NSECIF EVPSXE, V GTXGFT FVOTE JSPZ

SESRISPU, V NTTO XC TYSFOXTBN,

LZSFOBTE PZVP VBT LXBBIGPTBN: PZTU

ZVYT CXBNVWTE PZT FXBO, PZTU ZVYT

GBXYXWTO PZT ZXFU XET XC SNBVTF IEPX

VEKTB, PZTU VBT KXET VJVU DVLWJVBO.

Crossword: NUMBERS • By Rowan Millson

ACROSS

1 "... now the coat was without
   __" (John 19:23)
5 __ Aviv
8 Catch fly balls
12 Yen
13 Food label info
14 *The Ghost and Mrs.* __
15 Transfer
17 Letters meaning "King of
   the Jews"
18 Jesus (Heb. 1:6) (2 words)
20 Ill temper
21 Employs
22 Southwestern desert feature
25 Feel ill
26 Gaping hole
29 Jesus (Rev. 1:8) (3 words)
33 Tire pressure unit
34 Frigid
35 Grandson of Eve
36 Mock fanfare
38 Charged-up atom
40 Jesus (1 Cor.15:45, 47)
   (3 words)
46 Clods
47 Doubt-ridden
48 "We are __ men" (Gen. 42:31)
49 Hotshot
50 Pianist Gilels or actor Jannings
51 River deposit

52 "I do __ my bow in the cloud"
   (Gen. 9:13)
53 Quarrel

DOWN

1 Ride the waves
2 "I kiss'd thee __ kill'd thee"
   (*Othello*) (2 words)
3 "For this __ is mount Sinai in
   Arabia" (Gal. 4:25)
4 Savior of the world
5 One of twelve of Israel
6 "And Israel smote him with
   the __ of the sword" (Num. 21:24)
7 Lethargic
8 Strike forcefully
9 Esau and Nimrod
10 Suffix with million
11 Toothy look
16 Viola or cello (Abbr.)
19 Norwegian city
22 Atlas feature
23 Cid and Greco
24 Mean
25 Whatever
27 Sixth word of the Gettysburg
   Address
28 "For he __ numbered with us"
   (Acts 1:17)
30 Military assistant
31 These yield gum arabic

54

1	2	3	4		5	6	7		8	9	10	11
12					13				14			
15				16					17			
18								19				
			20					21				
22	23	24				25				26	27	28
29				30	31				32			
33				34					35			
		36	37				38	39				
40	41				42				43	44	45
46					47							
48					49				50			
51					52				53			

32 Threatens
37 Balance sheet entry
38 Graphic within 22-Down
39 Lyric poem
40 Toys for __
41 Mata __

42 "God hath spoken __; twice have I heard this" (Ps. 62:11)
43 Landfill site
44 Soprano's solo, perhaps
45 "... and every man's heart shall __" (Isa. 13:7)

55

Multiple Choice

1 What was engraved on the twelve stones
   on the breastplate of the high priest?

   A   The kings of Israel
   B   The names of the tribes of Israel
   C   Parables
   D   The Ten Commandments

2 Who upset his brothers by telling them of
   his dreams?

   A   Jacob
   B   Joseph
   C   Daniel
   D   Jesus

3 Who did God tell to name his son
   Mahershalalhashbaz?

   A   Hosea
   B   Jeremiah
   C   Isaiah
   D   Iddo

Word Search: MAKING THE TABERNACLE

```
M  T  A  E  S  Y  C  R  E  M  J  M  Z  L  S
N  M  S  R  E  T  I  P  A  H  C  T  L  A  T
Y  K  M  F  R  F  T  M  H  S  N  E  T  M  E
L  K  X  A  V  L  C  R  B  D  N  L  F  P  K
X  C  T  K  I  Q  T  R  U  N  T  R  Q  S  C
Y  L  W  N  X  T  A  R  F  O  N  A  C  T  O
A  R  E  J  C  N  I  M  T  M  C  C  L  A  S
V  N  D  Q  C  A  I  M  L  L  K  S  H  N  H
B  G  T  H  H  T  L  S  Y  A  P  H  F  D  K
N  O  E  T  T  R  D  B  R  V  V  L  D  J  Q
T  S  A  I  T  L  L  O  Y  A  T  E  M  B  E
T  O  H  R  H  Y  Q  W  M  R  L  K  R  H  T
G  S  Y  M  D  T  N  L  D  G  O  L  D  P  A
Q  D  N  T  J  S  Z  S  Q  H  L  Z  I  T  G
B  L  U  E  T  B  S  I  L  V  E  R  H  P  C
```

ALMONDS	COURT	MERCYSEAT
ALTAR	GATE	PILLARS
BLUE	GOAT HAIR	SCARLET
BOARDS	GOLD	SHITTIM
BOWLS	LAMPSTAND	SILVER
BRANCHES	LAVER	SOCKETS
CHAPITERS	LINEN	

Multiple Choice

1 Who had an unusual vision of one angel running to meet another?

    A Isaiah
    B Balaam
    C Zechariah
    D Seraiah

2 The ephod is an apron-like garment worn by whom?

    A The scapegoat
    B The high priest
    C Abraham
    D The cherubim

3 Who told Job that God would fill a righteous man with laughter?

    A Elihu
    B Zophar
    C Bildad
    D Eliphaz

Letter Squares: ESTHER 7:1

ITH	HE	QUE	TO	R T	QUE	AND	EN.
SO	NG	T W	THE	CA	HA	KI	ME
MAN	BAN	THE	ES				

Letter Squares: PSALMS 1:6

F T	Y O	SH .	HE	E L	ODL	HTE	Y S
RIG	FOR	HE	UT	KN	HAL	OWE	: B
L P	F T	OUS	WA	THE	WA	ORD	THE
UNG	ERI	TH	Y O	TH

Multiple Choice

1   All the priests come from what tribe of Israel?

    A   Judah
    B   Benjamin
    C   Levi
    D   Joseph

2   Who was the third son of Adam and Eve?

    A   Seth
    B   Jared
    C   Methuselah
    D   Lamech

3   Who constructed the first temple in Jerusalem?

    A   Joshua and Caleb
    B   Rehoboam and Jeroboam
    C   Solomon
    D   Zerubbabel and Joshua

Word Search: REBEKAH AND ISAAC

```
M D G W G R E T A W F O L L E W N
L R T L W B E T H U E L N M B V E
T T A K E A W I F E E T L R K Y D
P X Y D R I N K M Z E G O Y L Z I
H D W M K B Q W J S F T D H K D A
P G K A Y B K G O T H M E O E S M
M Q H H D O L R B E T L N T L L G
G M L A E R A R R L O D R R V E O
B T W R R N K F K V E A H M K M L
P R R B E J T H E L P S R P K A D
Z D B A V C M D F E T J S N V C R
Y R K W O T H G D N F R Z E L R I
F L J W C E C A A S I O M K D E N
K R T K R M N V K L G N O Z N T G
K K T S Z R R N K P H M M D T A T
N H J R O E R T L M Z R N Z M W G
N J R C S C D Z E C I O H C V N X
```

ABRAHAM
AROSE
BETHUEL
BLESSED
BORN
BROTHER
CHOICE

COSTLY
COVERED
DEPARTED
DRINK
FOOD
GOLD RING
HE LOVED HER

ISAAC
LODGE
MAIDEN
SERVANT
TAKE A WIFE
WATER CAMELS
WELL OF WATER

62

Verse Decoder: JOSHUA 1:2

HINT: In the puzzle below, the letter "J" is actually an "E."

EYSJS EL SJXCRKH GS FJRF; KYI HTJXJUYXJ

RXGSJ, VY YCJX HTGS MYXFRK, HTYN, RKF

RDD HTGS WJYWDJ, NKHY HTJ DRKF ITGQT

G FY VGCJ HY HTJE, JCJK HY HTJ QTGDFXJK

YU GSXRJD.

63

Crossword: BIBLICAL TRIBES · By Thomas W. Schier

ACROSS

1 Priest's garb
4 Rude look
8 "... they have made them a molten __" (Ex. 32:8)
12 Coffee, slangily
13 Kind of fall
14 "Dies __" (Latin hymn)
15 Advice columnist Landers
16 Tribe member in Matthew 10:4
18 "__, O ye nations, with his people" (Deut. 32:43)
20 Tribe in Acts 2:9
21 Comic Johnson
22 "And the Lord said unto __" (Gen. 4:15)
23 "Behold the __ of God" (John 1:29)
25 Punishes again, Singapore-style
29 "Who __ to judge?" (2 words)
30 Communion service item
32 Actress Gardner
33 "I will not __ his parts" (Job 41:12)
35 Hotfooted it
36 Giant Giant
37 1979 exiled Iranian
39 Open-jawed
42 Sovereign's staff
45 Tribe member in 2 Kings 17:29
47 Santa __, CA
48 "... and his voice will we __" (Josh. 24:24)
49 Fix a sock
50 Actor Chaney
51 Swampy bogs
52 Length x width, for a rectangle
53 Believer's suffix

DOWN

1 Open a bit
2 Solitary
3 Tribe in Numbers 13:9
4 Bibliography abbr.
5 "... the __ of God was upon him" (Luke 2:40)
6 Primrose path, literally
7 H, to Homer
8 Movie theater
9 Moistureless
10 "Even of __ my people is risen up" (Micah 2:8)
11 Professional charges
17 Oblong priestly vestment
19 Sphere
22 __ up (plenty perturbed)
23 Varnish ingredient
24 Latin 101 word
25 "Too-Ra-Loo-Ra-Loo-___"
26 Tribe in Numbers 1:43
27 Mother of Cain
28 "Why is thy spirit so __" (1 Kgs. 21:5)

1	2	3		4	5	6	7		8	9	10	11
12				13					14			
15				16				17				
18			19					20				
		21					22					
23	24					25				26	27	28
29				30	31					32		
33			34						35			
			36				37	38				
39	40	41				42					43	44
45					46					47		
48					49					50		
51					52					53		

30 He was originally called Simon
31 Back muscle, familiarly
34 Some health insurers' requirements
35 Tree trickling
37 Frighten
38 Salon shade

39 Dating from (2 words)
40 Actor Kaplan
41 Sermon finale
42 Magi's directional guide
43 Genesis son
44 Bombastic language
46 Wyo. neighbor

65

Letter Squares: PSALMS 6:4

RD,	THY	RET	ES'	SA	, O	OH	SAV
LIV	KE.	DE	OR	URN	L:		ME	RCI
E M	ER	SOU	MY	LO	E F		

Multiple Choice

1 Who led in the construction of the second temple?

   A Joshua and Caleb
   B Zerubbabel and Joshua
   C Asa and Abijam
   D Rehoboam and Jeroboam

2 Who was Jacob's father-in-law?

   A Samuel
   B Moses
   C Eleazar
   D Laban

3 God said that what city's cry was great and its sin very grievous?

   A Sodom
   B Rome
   C Egypt
   D Enoch

Word Search: JOHN THE BAPTIST

```
W  V  F  R  E  P  E  N  T  T  F  L  E  A  R  S  I
L  Z  B  F  D  M  P  R  E  A  C  H  I  N  G  G  F
F  S  T  K  X  L  T  H  Q  B  A  P  T  I  S  M  M
Q  S  G  M  K  E  B  X  E  F  W  K  Z  C  M  M  Z
T  E  W  K  N  G  T  H  B  R  R  A  R  N  C  R  Z
B  N  D  W  N  N  T  K  T  S  O  L  T  A  X  S  E
H  E  X  G  L  A  J  P  E  E  T  D  M  E  T  T  C
E  V  H  E  C  N  A  D  L  T  B  E  I  N  R  S  H
R  I  M  E  X  F  U  Y  T  R  L  A  L  A  R  U  A
O  G  G  M  A  T  N  E  L  H  E  T  Z  T  S  C  R
D  R  P  X  I  D  U  C  A  R  N  H  R  I  R  O  I
N  O  Q  T  J  Q  E  I  Y  E  W  B  T  Z  L  L  A
Z  F  L  R  N  Y  R  D  M  H  L  I  L  A  Y  E  H
G  U  R  A  M  J  N  R  O  J  R  R  M  C  E  N  K
M  G  B  R  T  L  A  N  K  D  X  T  Q  L  H  L  K
L  R  W  K  R  G  E  X  X  R  N  H  R  M  H  G  G
M  M  K  P  P  Y  Q  K  G  I  R  D  L  E  M  X  F
```

ANGEL
BANQUET
BAPTISM
BEHEADED
BIRTH
CAMEL HAIR
DANCE
ELIZABETH

FORGIVENESS
GARMENT
GIRDLE
HEROD
HERODIAS
HONEY
ISRAEL
LEATHER

LOCUSTS
MULTITUDES
PREACHING
REPENT
WATER
ZECHARIAH

Multiple Choice

1 What third king of Judah was also the
   great-grandson of Solomon?

   A Asa
   B Jehoiada
   C Josiah
   D Ahab

2 Which man was said to be an excellent
   speaker?

   A Aaron
   B Phinehas
   C Abiathar
   D Ahimelech

3 What priest dedicated the newly rebuilt
   walls of Jerusalem during Nehemiah's
   ministry?

   A Pashur
   B Eleazar
   C Zadok
   D Eliashib

Multiple Choice

1 The angel of the Lord appeared to what man and called him a mighty man of valor?

    A Gera
    B Gideoni
    C Gideon
    D Giddalti

2 Which of these men pulled down the Temple of Dagon?

    A Solomon
    B Salmon
    C Samson
    D Sargon

3 The prince of the eunuchs gave what man the name Shadrach?

    A Daniel
    B Mishael
    C Hananiah
    D Azariah

Letter Squares: PSALMS 7:1

T M	GO	PU	Y T	MY	O I	IN	ORD
T :	D ,	RUS	E D	THE	O L		

Verse Decoder: MICAH 1:4

HINT: In the puzzle below, the letter "G" is actually a "T."

TKZ GCU RDYKGTPKO OCTBB WU RDBGUK

YKZUL CPR, TKZ GCU ATBBUXO OCTBB WU

SBUVG, TO ITN WUVDLU GCU VPLU, TKZ TO

GCU ITGULO GCTG TLU EDYLUZ ZDIK T

OGUUE EBTSU.

Word Search: **WOMEN OF THE OLD TESTAMENT**

```
H   Z   H   N   O   A   D   A   I   H   D   V   M
P   A   B   A   H   A   R   O   H   A   G   A   R
E   Q   P   T   P   H   E   L   R   K   R   N   H
N   D   B   Z   T   N   H   M   J   P   K   B   A
I   M   H   U   I   F   T   W   N   N   A   K   K
N   A   R   A   Q   R   S   J   G   J   R   H   E
N   I   H   L   C   K   E   R   U   A   D   I   B
A   R   A   M   D   L   E   D   C   Y   M   P   E
H   I   N   L   Q   M   I   H   H   O   R   T   R
K   M   N   Z   O   T   E   M   A   P   L   G   C
W   G   A   G   H   L   P   N   K   G   N   B   R
K   P   H   A   R   U   T   E   K   Z   A   N   B
M   S   A   R   A   H   F   N   Y   B   K   R   J
```

ESTHER	MILCAH	RACHEL
GOMER	MIRIAM	RAHAB
HAGAR	NAOMI	REBEKAH
HANNAH	NOADAIH	RIZPAH
JUDITH	ORPAH	RUTH
KETURAH	PENINNAH	SARAH

Crossword: BIBLICAL BROWSING · By Barbara A. Marques

ACROSS

1 "__ not the earth, neither the sea" (Rev. 7:3)
5 Dad's day gift?
8 "... dove found no rest for the __ of her foot" (Gen. 8:9)
12 A duke of the Horites (Gen. 36:21)
13 Noah's overacting son?
14 "O Lord is against them that do __" (Ps. 34:16)
15 "And they tied unto it a __ of blue" (Ex. 39:31)
16 "God with us" (Matt. 1:23)
18 He ordered Christ's crucifixion
20 Grads
21 Commotion
22 Insect life stage
23 Letters of the Apostles
25 "Pass through the __, and command the people" (Josh. 1:11)
29 Goal
30 Sister
31 Small job to do
33 "... man should be alone; I will make him an __ for him" (Gen. 2:18)
36 Founder of the Hebrew race
38 __ in rooster
39 "I __ unto Caesar" (Acts 25:11)
42 Feeble-minded
45 Jesus anointed his eyes with clay (John 9:6)
47 U.S. Treasury Agent (abbr.)

48 "For all have sinned, and __ short of the glory of God" (Rom. 3:23)
49 Alter __
50 "... earth, where moth and __ doth corrupt" (Matt. 6:19)
51 "... there shall come a __ out of Jacob" (Num. 24:17)
52 "And the strong shall be as __" (Isa. 1:31)
53 Regarding (2 words)

DOWN

1 Make oneself useful
2 Father of Palal (Neh. 3:25)
3 Takes back
4 Tramples
5 "... thou art my God; early will I seek __" (Ps. 63:1)
6 "... Israel, __ hath sent me unto you" (Ex. 3:14) (2 words)
7 Disciples talked with Jesus on the road to __
8 Father of Judah (Neh. 11:9)
9 Reproductive cell
10 "... and see where thou hast not been __ with" (Jer. 3:2)
11 Norse deity who defeated Thor
17 Swiss mountain
19 Young child
22 Originally called Simon
23 "... hungry, give him bread to __" (Prov. 25:21)
24 Daughter of Ingrid Bergman
26 Philemon's slave
27 "And if any man will __ thee at the law" (Matt. 5:40)

1	2	3	4		5	6	7		8	9	10	11
12					13				14			
15					16			17				
18			19			20					
	21				22						
23	24							25	26	27	28
29								30			
31			32		33			34	35		
	36	37				38				
39	40	41				42			43	44
45					46			47			
48				49			50			
51				52			53			

28 Explosive
32 Sharper
33 "... take the __ of salvation, and the sword of the Spirit" (Eph. 6:17)
34 Coming before
35 Sacred meditation
37 Not good
39 Alphabet to a preschooler

40 Secret plan
41 Southern Arizona Indian
42 "... they shall be as white as __" (Isa. 1:18)
43 Persevere
44 Prefix meaning "within"
46 "Hast thou not heard long __ how I have done it" (2 Kings 19:25)

Letter Squares: PSALMS 104:32

| EAR | KET | T T | TH, | BLE | H O | HE | D I |
| TH: | LOO | AN | HE | REM | N T | | |

Multiple Choice

1 Which man's strength departed from him when his head was shaved?

    A Nathan
    B Bani
    C Samson
    D Daniel

2 Jacob built an altar to God in what city?

    A Damascus
    B Nazareth
    C Bethel
    D Tyre

3 Which patriarch of the Old Testament was revealed as a prophet to King Abimelech?

    A Isaac
    B Noah
    C Abraham
    D Jacob

Multiple Choice

1   Who was taken to Babylon and trained
    for the king's service?

        A   Haggai
        B   Amos
        C   Jeremiah
        D   Daniel

2   A ram in the bush once took which man's
    place?

        A   Ishmael
        B   Joseph
        C   Isaac
        D   Zebulun

3   Which man went from a pit to a palace?

        A   Jacob
        B   Elijah
        C   Benjamin
        D   Manasseh

Word Search: **PLAGUES OF EGYPT**

```
S  H  Z  D  Q  N  R  E  V  O  S  S  A  P  L
K  E  L  Y  A  S  L  A  V  E  R  Y  C  K  I
M  B  I  I  S  R  A  E  L  I  T  E  S  L  C
L  D  M  L  X  L  K  X  L  M  H  G  I  F  E
P  I  B  T  F  R  M  N  N  S  D  V  D  K  R
D  S  R  Q  L  T  Y  K  E  F  E  V  E  N  E
B  E  V  B  O  I  L  S  H  S  D  S  W  H  V
N  A  X  X  V  V  V  L  T  O  S  D  O  J  I
N  S  V  N  R  K  I  O  O  R  O  A  L  M  R
J  E  R  N  T  A  C  R  K  O  R  G  L  S  E
T  X  D  H  H  K  P  V  L  A  R  P  A  G  L
S  T  S  U  C  O  L  B  H  L  P  X  N  O  I
N  M  Y  C  S  M  P  P  D  V  A  Z  X  R  N
C  X  M  T  F  G  K  B  C  M  Z  M  J  F  R
K  K  M  N  R  O  B  T  S  R  I  F  B  N  N
```

ALLOWED
BLOOD
BOILS
DARKNESS
DISEASE
DOORPOST
FIRSTBORN

FLIES
FROGS
HAIL
ISRAELITES
LAMB
LICE
LIVESTOCK

LOCUSTS
MOSES
NILE RIVER
PASSOVER
PHARAOH
SLAVERY

Multiple Choice

1   Whose amazing coat caused tremendous envy among his brothers?

    A   Joseph's
    B   Daniel's
    C   Aaron's
    D   Jacob's

2   Joseph said, "... the man in whose hand the cup was found, he shall be my" what?

    A   King
    B   Brother
    C   Servant
    D   Betrayer

3   God made the first covenant with Noah. With whom did he make the second covenant?

    A   Adam
    B   Abraham
    C   Cain
    D   David

Letter Squares: 1 KINGS 1:33

TO	THE	O S	M,	I TH	U T	AID	YO
E W	SER	TS	TAK	THE	UN	ALS	OF
ORD	VAN	NG	HE	R L	KI	YOU	,

Multiple Choice

1 According to Psalms, what trees are broken by the power of God's voice?

    A The sycamore trees
    B The cedars of Lebanon
    C The lilies of the field
    D The palm trees

2 Who heard God speaking out of a whirlwind?

    A Elisha
    B Nathan
    C Ahab
    D Job

3 What Hebrew captive interpreted the dreams of the Egyptian Pharaoh?

    A Jacob
    B Moses
    C Joseph
    D Reuben

Column Phrase: JEREMIAH 29:12

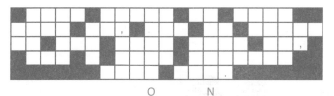

```
            O       N
P   A       NIAN    HU          HE
  TON     IUPAAL    UETCAEN
GONENDEHTLYYYYAOKMA
UAHDNMSWRLLDOEERSLLLL
```

Crossword: BEASTS OF PREY · By Rowan Millson

ACROSS

1 Norman of golf
5 "And after the __ Satan entered into him" (John 13:27)
8 "Be still, ye inhabitants of the __" (Isa. 23:2)
12 Not far
13 Flightless bird down under
14 "And the Lord spake unto Gad, David's __" (1 Chron. 21:9)
15 Sea between Italy and Albania
17 Healing mark
18 "... and the __ them, and scattereth the sheep" (John 10:12) (2 words)
20 "__ fi fo fum"
21 Three, on a sundial
22 Word with trust or social
25 __ and outs
26 What Joseph was cast into
29 "The old __ for lack of prey" (Job 4:11) (2 words)
33 Tree with tough, useful wood
34 Santa __, CA
35 "Take, thine __, eat, drink and be merry" (Luke 12:19)
36 "... he planteth an __" (Isa. 44:14)
37 Jetted bath
39 "And the beast which I saw was like __" (Rev. 13:2) (3 words)
45 Gemstone
46 Slight sleepwear
47 __ cloud in the sky (2 words)
48 Pigeon sound
49 Sisters
50 A book in *The Book of Mormon*
51 They're between ems and ohs
52 Chicken man, in the circus

DOWN

1 "... they __ not the bones till the morrow" (Zeph. 3:3)
2 Perform again
3 Viscount's superior
4 Merv of TV fame
5 Stiff bristles
6 Overlook
7 "Turandot" composer
8 First-generation Japanese immigrant
9 Split-off group
10 Rachel's sister
11 "It is a people that do __ in their heart" (Ps. 95:10)
16 Good serve
19 "... and shall __ at all the plagues thereof" (Jer. 49:17)
22 Ginger __ (soft drink)
23 Zip
24 Double this for a drum
25 One of David's captains
26 Small vegetable
27 __ *a Wonderful Life*

1	2	3	4		5	6	7		8	9	10	11
12					13				14			
15				16					17			
18							19					
		20				21						
22	23	24			25				26	27	28
29				30	31			32			
33				34				35			
		36				37	38				
	39	40				41			42	43	44
45					46						
47					48				49			
50					51				52			

28 Popular title starter
30 El __, Texas
31 Add some pizzazz to
32 A __ spoonful
36 Map book
37 Lily varieties
38 Warsaw is its cap.
39 "Take my yoke __ you" (Matt. 11:29)
40 Org. celebrating 50 years in 1999
41 Juan Ponce de __
42 Feverish condition
43 Actress Russo
44 Schoolroom fixture
45 "And the whole earth was of __ language" (Gen. 11:1)

Word Search: JONAH AND THE WHALE

```
T  R  C  A  P  T  A  I  N  M  L  K  J  M  V  M  B
H  H  P  H  C  C  M  T  C  R  R  D  E  Y  A  R  P
R  Y  J  D  T  A  R  S  H  I  S  H  R  T  W  Y  Q
O  D  N  W  R  F  S  P  V  Y  Y  G  M  O  N  L  E
W  X  L  E  T  O  A  T  Y  Y  R  J  L  T  R  M  C
N  G  N  K  C  I  L  L  L  E  K  L  T  P  D  H  I
D  V  T  G  D  N  L  L  A  O  A  F  D  N  R  N  F
D  P  H  F  T  E  E  T  N  W  T  X  R  I  A  T  I
W  W  A  X  B  N  F  S  S  H  X  S  Y  N  O  H  R
N  R  N  X  N  I  P  M  E  K  X  F  L  E  B  R  C
E  R  O  D  S  Y  E  T  A  R  T  M  A  V  R  E  A
V  L  J  H  L  R  E  F  E  R  P  T  N  E  E  E  S
R  T  F  X  A  M  L  L  Q  M  I  Z  D  H  V  D  T
N  J  R  P  Q  M  S  L  T  J  P  N  B  T  O  A  N
Y  K  P  L  M  Q  A  R  J  V  K  E  E  L  Z  Y  Q
T  O  C  D  N  I  W  T  A  E  R  G  S  R  L  S  F
J  M  A  D  E  V  O  W  S  V  M  N  F  T  S  D  B
```

ASLEEP	JOPPA	PRESENCE
BELLY	LORD	SACRIFICE
CAPTAIN	MADE VOWS	SWALLOW
CAST LOTS	MARINERS	TARSHISH
DRY LAND	NINEVEH	TEMPEST
GREAT FISH	OVERBOARD	THREE DAYS
GREAT WIND	PAID FARE	THROWN
JONAH	PRAYED	

Multiple Choice

1 What wise king made an alliance with Egypt when he married the pharaoh's daughter?

   A Jeroboam II
   B Solomon
   C Menahem
   D Saul

2 What book mentions a woman who plants a vineyard with her own hands?

   A Genesis
   B Proverbs
   C Joshua
   D Ecclesiastes

3 What king of Moab sent the prophet Balaam to curse Israel?

   A Balak
   B Ahaziah
   C Pharaoh
   D Saul

Letter Squares: ISAIAH 1:8

TH	AS	R	O	E	D	IS	ION	A	RD,
HTE	OTT	F	Z	IN	AUG	LE	FT	VIN
AGE	EYA	A C	AND

Multiple Choice

1 Which of these men made his dwelling
   place in Uz?

   A Job
   B Peter
   C Moses
   D John

2 Who was Elisha's servant?

   A Elijah
   B Gehazi
   C Caleb
   D Naaman

3 Which man hid himself from God
   because he was naked?

   A Adam
   B Abraham
   C John
   D Jesus

Multiple Choice

1   Who was crippled when a servant
    woman dropped him as a baby?

    A   Balaam
    B   Saul's brother
    C   Mephibosheth
    D   Jonathan's grandson

2   Which man pursued the life of David
    because of jealousy?

    A   David
    B   Zimri
    C   Saul
    D   Pekah

3   Who was so disgraced when Absalom
    did not follow his counsel that he hanged
    himself?

    A   Ahitophel
    B   Amnon
    C   Hushi
    D   Joab

Column Phrase: ISAIAH 59:1

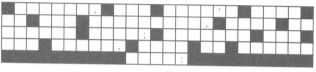

```
     A      OT          EE   RT            T  I
   E B R H O T   S H T H T H A O R T   T H H A I D
   I A E N H E A S A O H T E L E D D H S C A H N O T
   C S N N O L D V Y V R E A N E I I T E R A N N S T
```

Verse Decoder: PSALMS 101:1

HINT: In the puzzle below, the letter "I" is actually an "A."

I RYIVGY EP UBG IPPXSFUGH, ABGD BG SQ

EZGYABGXOGH, IDH RECYGUB ECU BSQ

FEORXISDU MGPEYG UBG XEYH. BGIY OV

RYIVGY, E XEYH, IDH XGU OV FYV FEOG

CDUE UBGG.

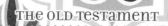

Word Search: THE SPIRIT VS. THE FLESH

```
P Y F R W O R S H I P K Y R G L
X T T K E T T M C X L P F K X R
Y I S L W M F X T G Q E M V F L
P N U P T D A N G M Q A N B X B
P A R C D V E H T B M C X J V D
A V T E K L Q C S F S E T T L E
H J T H L W O E E S N F H N M S
H O P E P I T V E I F U F O T I
W L M R B A U N E T T L T C N R
H M I B H R R G L V H I B P L E
Y D R L L E X T K T O F N R K L
E Y C W T G N P A N L F V K Y W
G D N T Q N W R S C O U R A G E
M L I F M A W M G K F E I R G L
L B G N I C I O J E R D T B X K
Q S U F F E R I N G B B Q W X Y
```

ANGER	GUILE	REJOICING
BITTERNESS	HAPPY	SHAME
COURAGE	HATE	SUFFERING
DECEIT	HOPE	TRUST
DESIRE	LOVE	VANITY
EMOTIONS	PEACEFUL	WORSHIP
GRIEF	PRIDE	WRATH

Crossword: BIBLICAL VESSELS · By Rowan Millson

ACROSS

1 Norwegian king
5 Group of wise guys
8 "... and ye shall __ no longer" (Ex. 9:28)
12 "Even as __ obeyed Abraham" (1 Peter 3:6)
13 Brian of Roxy Music
14 Opera solo
15 Communicator
17 Cot
18 "Thy navel is like __" (Song of Sol. 7:2) (3 words)
20 They can get personal
21 A sworded affair
22 "... and if any __ hath cleaved to mine hands" (Job 31:7)
25 "... and I will __ evil beasts out of the land" (Lev. 26:6)
26 Sound of surprise
29 "You anoint my head with oil; __" (Ps. 23:5) (shortened) (3 words)
33 "They are __ with the showers of the mountains" (Job 24:8)
34 Charged atom
35 Word of action
36 Lhasa __
38 "Out of whose womb came the __ ?" (Job 38:29)
40 "For now we see through __" (1 Cor. 13:12) (3 words)

45 Plant mixed with myrrh in John 19:39
46 Ta-ta
47 Singer Horne
48 Allen-wrench shape
49 7-Down's Prince
50 For fear that
51 Thing, on deeds
52 Italian princely family

DOWN

1 Mountain in Thessaly
2 Animal shelter
3 Jason's ship
4 New Hebrides, today
5 Pinochle combos
6 NASA pressure unit
7 "Polovtsian Dances" composer
8 Luxurious fur
9 Sweetheart (2 words)
10 "__ Misbehavin'"
11 Talk like an ox?
16 So-so connection
19 "... and brought forth __" (Num. 17:8)
22 Mercedes rival
23 Soap component
24 Stop-sign shapes
25 "... many shall __ to and fro" (Dan. 12:4)
27 "... consider __ ways, and be wise" (Prov. 6:6)

94

1	2	3	4		5	6	7		8	9	10	11
12					13				14			
15				16					17			
18								19				
			20				21					
22	23	24				25				26	27	28
29				30	31				32			
33				34					35			
		36	37				38	39				
	40					41				42	43	44
45					46							
47					48				49			
50					51				52			

28 Symbol of royal power
30 Leaning Tower locale
31 Barnyard strutter
32 Rest upon
37 Dress feature
38 "Turn ye not unto __" (Lev. 19:4)
39 Heel

40 Away from a weather
41 One and only
42 Casks
43 Plunder
44 Yesteryear
45 The whole enchilada

Multiple Choice

1 Who built a city called Enoch east of Eden?

    A Cain
    B Adam
    C Noah
    D Abram

2 Who persuaded the clever woman of Tekoah to pretend to be a widow in order to play on King David's sympathy?

    A Joab
    B Uzzie
    C Tobiah
    D Hemam

3 Which of these men was killed with a stone?

    A Goliath
    B Samson
    C David
    D Methuselah

Letter Squares: ISAIAH 4:2

OUS	BR	ORI	H O	TIF	AY	AND	LOR
THE	T D	GL	HE	EAU	THA	E B	D B
SHA	ANC	F T	UL	LL	IN	,	

Word Search: JOB'S SORROW

```
N  Z  O  P  H  A  R  S  T  N  A  V  R  E  S
L  N  Q  H  B  B  L  A  M  E  L  E  S  S  D
R  N  J  X  S  H  T  S  B  D  N  V  M  A  M
S  Z  R  A  R  T  N  A  F  M  K  N  D  T  N
T  E  T  A  L  D  E  B  D  K  R  L  H  M  C
P  A  N  X  M  G  M  E  Z  P  I  G  K  A  W
N  E  T  U  R  S  T  A  A  B  I  X  M  J  O
K  L  E  W  T  R  N  N  H  R  B  E  L  L  R
C  R  R  H  N  R  I  S  P  L  L  D  L  M  S
N  W  F  X  S  V  O  U  I  S  O  X  E  N  H
N  E  G  B  Y  Q  P  F  L  M  B  D  J  B  I
R  L  N  E  Z  H  P  V  E  R  C  O  N  U  P
H  S  N  R  F  L  A  W  T  L  J  M  I  L  E
K  O  S  N  A  E  D  L  A  H  C  K  L  L  D
M  S  U  F  F  E  R  I  N  G  C  K  M  S  S
```

APPOINTMENT	ELIPHAZ	SERVANTS
BILDAD	FORTUNES	SHEEP
BLAMELESS	MONEY	SLEW
BOILS	OXEN	SUFFERING
BULLS	RAMS	UPRIGHT
CAMELS	SABEANS	WORSHIPED
CHALDEANS	SATAN	ZOPHAR

Multiple Choice

1 Where did Lot make his home?

    A Enoch
    B Rome
    C Corinth
    D Sodom

2 Who made numerous attempts to swindle Jacob, and ultimately prospered?

    A Joseph
    B Laban
    C Reuben
    D Mizpah

3 Where did the prostitute Rahab live?

    A Medes
    B Persia
    C Jericho
    D Sodom

Multiple Choice

1   How many of Joseph's brothers went to
    Egypt to buy grain?

        A   12
        B   10
        C   11
        D   6

2   Who was the youngest son of Jacob?

        A   Reuben
        B   Benjamin
        C   Levi
        D   Judah

3   How many days was Jonah in the belly of
    the great fish?

        A   3
        B   14
        C   20
        D   1

Letter Squares: AMOS 3:3

TO	TW	PT	O W	HER	ED?	CAN	GET
GRE	, E	THE	Y B	E	A	XCE	ALK

Word Search:
MEN FOUND IN THE OLD TESTAMENT

```
F Y L N H Y K V B M M Z Q Q T L A
T J C A I H C A L A M V F K Y E H
Q M N N K D D N J H B A G Y R O S
V O J W Y A I E X A H N H K D J I
J H B N N S R T S R K Q M T M Q L
T M X I A E F O J B R H R B A B E
D L E A M K L R K A J P A T F O C
J L C I B O W A N T F L V J B A J
U N A J M W B K Z A R A M H I Z T
D H B O O S F H K O P G R O N L B
A D N J K S E L A C R X K S L L E
S J R Q K Q H S H G T K N E N Q J
D I V A D K F U O C G D Z A G N L
H L E A M H S I A M U A W N F X M
B H Z X J L T J A I B J I R N T Z
N O M L A S J D L G R J O S E P H
W Q N H T T A E M N E Z E K I E L
```

ABRAHAM	ELIUD	JONAH
ADAM	EZEKIEL	JOSEPH
ARAM	HAGGAI	JOSHUA
AZOR	HOSEA	JUDAS
BOAZ	ISAAC	MALACHI
DANIEL	ISHMAEL	MOSES
DAVID	JEREMIAH	SALMON
ELIJAH	JOATHAM	SOLOMON
ELISHA	JOEL	

102

pocket posh® king james puzzles

SOLUTIONS

SOLUTIONS

1.
Thus saith the LORD; For three transgressions of Gaza, and for four, I will not turn away the punishment thereof; because they carried away captive the whole captivity, to deliver them up to Edom:

3.

2.

H	E	L	M			A	F	T			C	R	A	B
A	R	I	A			B	R	A			R	A	R	E
H	I	S	R	E	C	O	M	P	E	N	C	E		
S	N	A	I	L			M	E	A	D				
			M	I	D			C	O	M	E	T		
S	N	O	B		R	O	S	E			A	N	A	
I	A	M	A	G	A	I	N	S	T	Y	O	U		
A	M	I		U	G	L	I			H	O	S	T	
M	E	T	A	L				P	A	R				
			L	A	K	E			D	I	A	L	S	
T	H	O	U	G	H	T	S	O	F	M	A	N		
W	A	R	M			A	N	T			T	O	T	O
A	M	E	S			N	A	Y			S	K	E	W

4.
1. A   2. B   C. 3

5.
Yet in this thing ye did not believe the LORD your God,

6.

1. A   2. B   3. C

7.

1. B   2. B   3. C

8.

9.

Hear, O Israel: The LORD
our God is one LORD:

10.

And that whosoever would
not come within three days,
according to the counsel of the
princes and the elders, all his
substance should be forfeited,
and himself separated from
the congregation of those that
had been carried away.

11.

SOLUTIONS

12.
1. A 2. D 3. A

13.

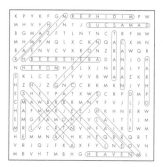

14.
But the salvation of the
righteous is of the Lord:
he is their strength in
the time of trouble.

15.
1. D 2. B 3. D

16.
1. C 2. A 3. B

17.
All the congregation of
Israel shall keep it.

18.

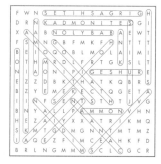

19.

Then the LORD said unto Moses, now shalt thou see what I will do to Pharaoh: For with a strong hand shall he let them go, and with a strong hand shall he drive them out of his land.

21.

So they took up Jonah, and cast him forth into the sea:

22.

1. D   2. A   3. C

20.

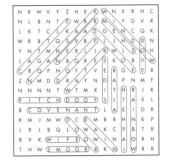

23.

SOLUTIONS

24.
1. B   2. B   3. C

25.
1. D   2. A   3. B

26.
Many are the afflictions of the righteous: but the Lord delivereth him out of them all.

27.

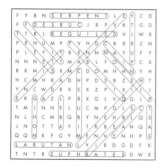

28.
And it came to pass, when they had eaten up the corn which they had brought out of Egypt, their Father said unto them, go again, buy us a little food.

29.

1 S	2 L	3 A	4 M		5	6 S	P	7 A		8 S	9 H	10 E	11 M

(crossword grid)

30.
Then said the LORD, Doest thou well to be angry?

109

solutions

31.

35.

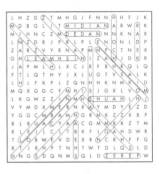

32.
1. C   2. A   3. B

33.
And now, O ye priests, this commandment is for you.

34.
1. B   2. C   3. C

36.
And he dreamed, and behold a ladder set up on the earth, and the top of it reached to heaven: And behold the angels of God ascending and descending on it.

37.
For I am the LORD, I change not;

SOLUTIONS

38.

S	L	A	P		I	A	N		A	P	S	E
H	A	I	R		F	L	O		R	O	A	N
U	N	D	E	R	S	T	A	N	D	I	N	G
T	A	S	T	Y		O	H	I	O			
			Z	E	D			G	R	A	P	H
A	C	N	E		Y	E	A	H		L	E	A
S	H	A	L	L	A	N	Y	T	E	A	C	H
P	I	P		E	D	D	A		A	S	K	S
S	T	E	R	N		H	A	S				
			A	T	O	P		D	I	A	N	A
O	F	G	O	O	D	A	N	D	E	V	I	L
L	I	E	U		O	V	A		S	E	L	L
D	E	L	L		R	E	B		T	R	E	Y

39.

40.

1. B   2. B   3. B

41.

As far as the east is from the west, so far hath he removed our transgressions from us.

42.

1. B   2. C   3. B

43.

1. C   2. B   3. C

44.

Alas for the day! For the day of the Lord is at hand.

111

45.

(word search solution grid)

47.

(crossword solution grid)

46.

Ah sinful nation, a people laden with iniquity, a seed of evildoers, children that are corrupters: They have forsaken the LORD, they have provoked the Holy One of Israel unto anger, they are gone away backward.

48.

1. B   2. B   3. C

SOLUTIONS

49.

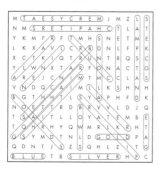

52.

For the Lord knoweth the way of the righteous: but the way of the ungodly shall perish.

53.

1. C   2. A   3. D

50.

1. C   2. B   3. C

54.

51.

So the king and Haman came to banquet with Esther the queen.

113

solutions

55.

Moses my servant is dead;
now therefore arise, go over
this Jordon, thou, and all this
people, unto the land which
I do give to them, even to
the Children of Israel.

57.

Return, O LORD, deliver
my soul: oh save me for
thy mercies' sake.

58.

1. A   2. D   3. A

56.

A	L	B		O	G	L	E		C	A	L	F
J	O	E		P	R	A	T		I	R	A	E
A	N	N		C	A	N	A	A	N	I	T	E
R	E	J	O	I	C	E		M	E	D	E	S
		A	R	T	E		H	I	M			
L	A	M	B		R	E	C	A	N	E	S	
A	M	I		P	L	A	T	E		A	V	A
C	O	N	C	E	A	L		S	P	E	D	
			O	T	T		S	H	A	H		
A	G	A	P	E		S	C	E	P	T	E	R
S	A	M	A	R	I	T	A	N		A	N	A
O	B	E	Y		D	A	R	N		L	O	N
F	E	N	S		A	R	E	A		I	S	T

59.

SOLUTIONS

60.
1. A   2. A   3. D

61.
1. C   2. C   3. C

62.
O LORD my God, in thee
do I put my trust:

63.
And the mountains shall be
molten under him, and the
valleys shall be cleft, as wax
before the fire, and as the
waters that are poured
down a steep place.

64.

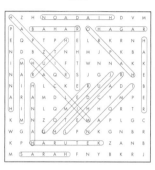

65.

¹H	²U	³R	⁴T		⁵T	⁶I	⁷E		⁸S	⁹O	¹⁰L	¹¹E

(crossword grid)

115

66.
He looketh on the earth,
and it trembleth:

67.
1. C   2. C   3. C

68.
1. D   2. C   3. D

69.

70.
1. A   2. C   3. B

71.
The king also said unto them,
Take with you the servants
of your lord,

72.
1. B   2. D   3. C

73.
Then shall ye call upon me, and
ye shall go and pray unto me,
and I will hearken unto you.

74.

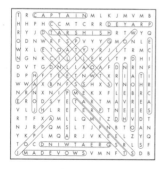

75.

76.
1. B 2. B 3. A

77.
And the daughter of Zion is left as a cottage in a vineyard,...

78.
1. A 2. B 3. A

79.
1. C 2. C 3. A

80.
Behold, the LORD's hand is not shortened, that it cannot save; neither his ear heavy, that it cannot hear:

81.

A prayer of the afflicted, when he is overwhelmed, and poureth out his compliant before the Lord. Hear my prayer, O LORD, and let my cry come unto thee.

82.

83.

84.

1. A   2. A   3. A

85.

In that day shall the branch of the LORD be beautiful and glorious

SOLUTIONS

86.

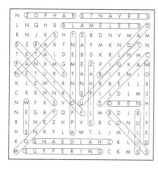

87.
1. D   2. B   3. C

88.
1. B   2. B   3. A

89.
Can two walk together,
except they be agreed?

90.

SOLUTIONS

86.

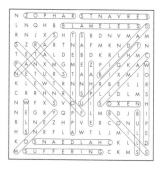

87.
1. D   2. B   3. C

88.
1. B   2. B   3. A

89.
Can two walk together,
except they be agreed?

90.

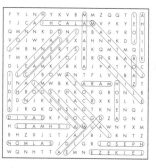

COLLECT ALL TITLES IN THIS SERIES!